SUPER STEM CAREERS

A Day at Work with a
SOFTWARE
DEVELOPER

DEVON MCKINNEY

PowerKiDS
press.

New York

Published in 2016 by The Rosen Publishing Group, Inc.
29 East 21st Street, New York, NY 10010

First Edition

Editor: Caitie McAneney
Book Design: Katelyn Heinle/Reann Nye

Photo Credits: Cover shapecharge/E+/Getty Images; cover, pp. 1, 3, 4, 6, 8, 10–14, 16–20, 22–24 (circuit vector design) VLADGRIN/Shutterstock.com; p. 5 (top) Dragon Images/Shutterstock.com; p. 5 (bottom) wavebreakmedia/Shutterstock.com; p. 7 Goodluz/Shutterstock.com; p. 9 (top) Morrowind/Shutterstock.com; p. 9 (bottom) Mclek/Shutterstock.com; p. 11 Tyler Olson/Shutterstock.com; p. 13 Rido/ Shutterstock.com; p. 15 (top) Denys Prykhodov/Shutterstock.com; p. 15 (bottom) Brian A Jackson/Shutterstock.com; p. 17 (algorithm) https://en.wikipedia.org/wiki/ File-Diagram_for_the_computation_of_Bernoulli_numbers.jpg; p. 17 (Lovelace) https://commons.wikimedia.org/wiki/File-Ada Lovelace portrait jpg; p. 18 Syda Productions/Shutterstock.com; p. 19 Stephen VanHorn/Shutterstock.com; p. 21 dotshock/Shutterstock.com; p. 22 YanLev/Shutterstock.com.

Library of Congress Cataloging-in-Publication Data

McKinney, Devon.
 A day at work with a software developer / Devon McKinney.
      pages cm. — (Super STEM careers)
 Includes index.
 ISBN 978-1-5081-4414-4 (pbk.)
 ISBN 978-1-5081-4415-1 (6 pack)
 ISBN 978-1-5081-4416-8 (library binding)
 1. Computer software—Development—Vocational guidance—Juvenile literature. I. Title.
 QA76.76.D47M3973 2016
 005.3023—dc23
                          2015027137

Manufactured in the United States of America

CONTENTS

MAKING COMPUTERS WORK

Imagine you have a computer in front of you, but it doesn't work. The computer itself—or hardware—is in good shape, but it can't carry out tasks. You can't play games or watch videos or even surf the Internet. What's this computer missing? Software!

Software is the programs that run on computers and carry out certain functions, or tasks. It makes the computer work. Because of software, the possibilities for computer functions are endless. However, software **developers** need to create the software first. It's their job to think of useful and fun ways our computers can work for us.

In their work, software developers use "STEM," which stands for "science, **technology**, **engineering**, and math."

COMPUTER SCIENCE

Software developers study and practice computer science. You may have heard of biology, chemistry, and physics, which are all branches of science. They all deal with the laws of nature.

However, computer science is a little different. It's the science of information processes and the way they **interact** with the world. People who work in computer science are called computer scientists. They use computers to **implement** new ways to pass on information. Like many scientists, computer scientists look at how one thing can lead to another. For example, one set of instructions can be followed to make a computer do a certain task.

Unlike many scientists, computer scientists don't work in a lab. They often work in offices.

COMPUTER TECHNOLOGY

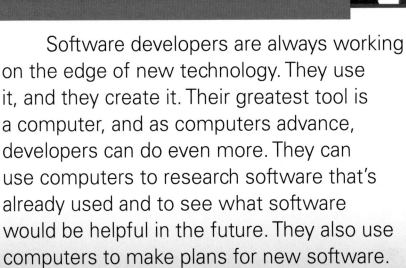

Software developers are always working on the edge of new technology. They use it, and they create it. Their greatest tool is a computer, and as computers advance, developers can do even more. They can use computers to research software that's already used and to see what software would be helpful in the future. They also use computers to make plans for new software. They can share ideas and communicate with other developers through email and video chatting.

Most importantly, software developers can start implementing their software idea. This is called computer programming. They have to **translate** their idea into a code, or programming language, that computers can understand.

SUPER STEM SMARTS

Popular programming languages include Java, C++, and Python.

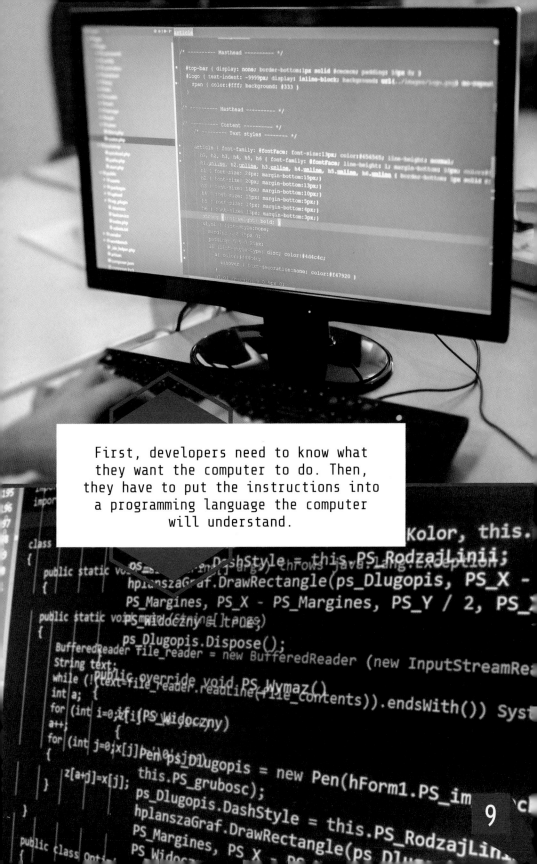

First, developers need to know what they want the computer to do. Then, they have to put the instructions into a programming language the computer will understand.

CODING TOOLS

Software developers need to know how to write computer programs, which is also called coding. Professional software developers are **experts** in programming languages. Coding technology isn't just for the experts, though. You can learn to code, too. There are plenty of tools to help beginners learn to create their own software.

Scratch is a programming language designed for students eight to 16 years old. This Web-based program uses graphics, or visuals, to help students understand programming. Students drag blocks into a workspace to make characters move. Hopscotch is an iPad **application** (app) that also uses visual programming to help students learn coding basics.

Programs such as Scratch and Hopscotch are also examples of software. Existing software can help us create new software!

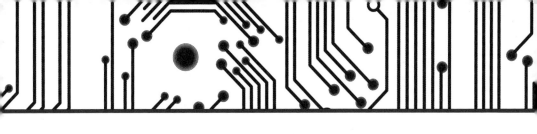

CODING TOOLS FOR BEGINNERS

Hopscotch
iPad app
visual programming
language

Tynker
Web
teaches programming
with lesson plans

Scratch
Web
visual programming
language

GameStar Mechanic
Web
users **design** their own
video games

Hackety Hack
Web
teaches basics of
programming with
Ruby language

Move the Turtle
iPad app
teaches programming
basics through a
colorful game

SOFTWARE ENGINEERING

"Engineering" means using math and science to solve problems. Engineers create new products and processes to make our lives easier. Software developers create new software as part of their job every day.

How do software developers start creating something? First, they need to look at the software that's out there. What does it do? What doesn't it do? Then, they come up with an idea for a new kind of software. They could also improve software that already exists. Software developers are good problem solvers because they study the problems that exist in current software and then develop a solution.

SUPER STEM SMARTS

Have you ever used a smartphone? There are many apps for smartphones that help people find directions, share pictures, and even exercise. Software developers come up with new apps all the time!

Designing software is a big part of a software developer's job. They need to think of how each part of the computer program will fit together to make it easy to use.

THE INTERNET OF THINGS

Imagine a world where your refrigerator sends a reminder to your phone to go grocery shopping. Imagine the road your parents are driving on telling their car it's icy. This kind of machine-to-machine communication is a part of the Internet of Things—the next big idea in software development.

Today, some software developers are engineering software that uses the data from **sensors** in an endless amount of products. Dog collars, televisions, and even refrigerators are all part of the growing Internet of Things. Software developers find new uses for this data all the time. It can even be sent to other devices, such as smartphones.

SUPER STEM SMARTS

The Internet of Things will connect objects and devices and help them work together to make people's lives easier.

Software developers will be responsible for turning nearly every object into a "smart" device. They'll have to come up with software that runs each computing device.

SOFTWARE AND MATH

Ada Lovelace is credited with being the world's first computer programmer. She invented the first software. Her work is also a great example of how math and software development come together.

Born in 1815, Lovelace grew up with a strong education in math and science. She was introduced to an inventor named Charles Babbage who had created a machine that could solve math problems, called the Analytical Engine. It's considered the first mechanical computer. Lovelace created an **algorithm** to make the machine **calculate** numbers. As a great mathematician, Lovelace used her problem-solving skills to figure out how to make the machine work.

SUPER STEM SMARTS

An algorithm is a set of steps that are followed to solve something. Some algorithms are used to solve math problems, while others complete a computer process.

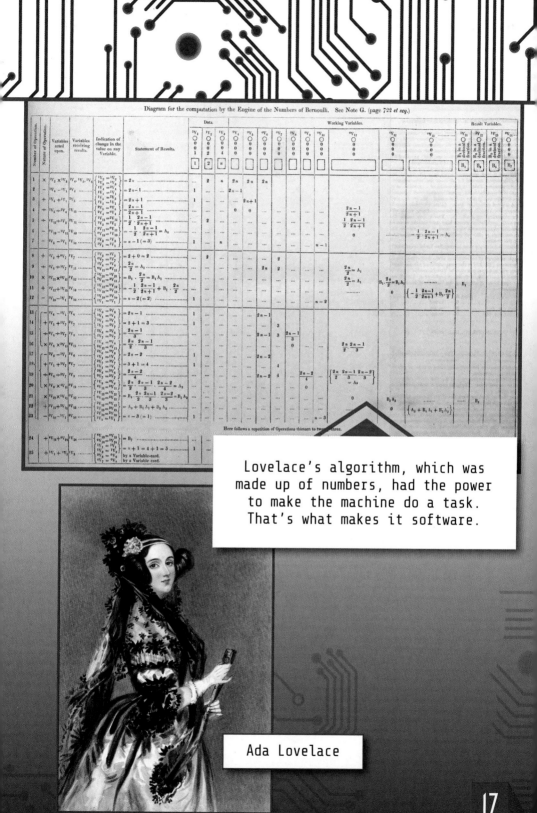

Lovelace's algorithm, which was made up of numbers, had the power to make the machine do a task. That's what makes it software.

Ada Lovelace

17

Math is a huge part of writing code, which is a key part of creating software. In programming, you have to create a step-by-step code so the computer knows exactly what to do. Writing code is a lot like doing algebra. Algebra is a kind of math that uses symbols, such as letters, to represent variables, which are numbers that change depending on the situation.

In Boolean algebra, the relationship between numbers can be expressed by only two values: 1 (true) or 0 (false). These values tell a computer when to perform a function. In other words, programmers use Boolean **logic** to tell computers what to do.

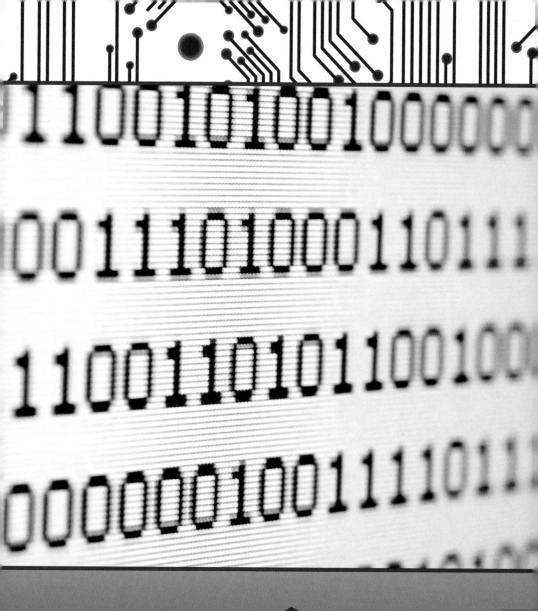

Software developers need to understand Boolean logic to understand how to solve problems in code.

A DAY IN THE LIFE

What's it like to work as a software developer? Most spend their day in an office. They work in many different settings—from the government to the military to private companies. Many software developers work for software publishers, or companies that design or acquire new software and put it on the market.

On a normal day, a software developer may research their users' needs through online data. Then, they'll design or plan new software. They also test software to see if it works. A software developer might also create a **diagram** to show programmers how to write the code for certain software.

SUPER STEM SMARTS

Each software developer's job is different because they work on different kinds of programs. Some develop fitness apps, while others create medical software.

Software developers may have meetings with other computer specialists to make sure their software idea will work well with existing technology.

BECOMING A SOFTWARE DEVELOPER

Do you have ideas for new computer programs? Do you love STEM and creating new things?

First, take as many math and science classes as you can. When you get to high school, take computer and technology classes. You're never too young to start coding classes through community programs. An **aspiring** software developer has to complete a bachelor's degree. Some get their degree in software engineering, while others study computer science or mathematics. It's smart to also get a master's degree and even specialize in a certain area, such as medicine or finance. With a career in software development, you'll create the technology of the future!

GLOSSARY

algorithm: A set of steps that are followed in order to solve a mathematical problem or complete a computer process.

application: A program that performs one of the major tasks for which a computer is used.

aspiring: Strongly wanting to achieve a goal.

calculate: To find the solution to a problem using math processes.

design: To create the plan for something.

developer: A person who creates something, such as computer software.

diagram: A drawing that explains or shows the parts of something or how something works.

engineering: The use of science and math to build better objects.

expert: Someone who has a special skill or knowledge.

implement: To begin to do or use something.

interact: To act together.

logic: The science that studies the formal processes used in thinking and reasoning.

sensor: A device that senses heat, light, motion, sound, or smells.

technology: The way people do something using tools and the tools that they use.

translate: To change words from one language into another language.

INDEX

WEBSITES

Due to the changing nature of Internet links, PowerKids Press has developed an online list of websites related to the subject of this book. This site is updated regularly. Please use this link to access the list: www.powerkidslinks.com/ssc/softw